Myths and legends of ancient
Britain and Ireland.

Famous Myths and Legends of the World

Myths and Legends of
ANCIENT BRITAIN
AND IRELAND

WORLD
BOOK

a Scott Fetzer company
Chicago
www.worldbook.com

World Book, Inc.
180 North LaSalle Street
Suite 900
Chicago, Illinois 60601
USA

For information about other World Book publications, visit our website at **www.worldbook.com** or call **1-800-967-5325**.

Library of Congress Cataloging-in-Publication Data

Myths and legends of ancient Britain and Ireland.
    pages cm. -- (Famous myths and legends of the world)
    Summary: "Myths and legends from ancient Britain and Ireland. Features include information about the history and culture behind the myths, pronunciations, lists of deities, word glossary, further information, and index"--Provided by publisher.
    Includes index.
    ISBN 978-0-7166-2637-4
    1. Mythology, Celtic--Juvenile literature. 2. Celts--Folklore--Juvenile literature. 3. Britons--Folklore--Juvenile literature. 4. Scots--Folklore--Juvenile literature. 5. Ireland--Folklore--Juvenile literature. 6. Wales--Folklore--Juvenile literature. 7. Scotland--Folklore--Juvenile literature. I. World Book, Inc. II. Series: Famous myths and legends of the world.
    BL900.M98 2015
    398.209415--dc23
                        2015014760

Set ISBN: 978-0-7166-2625-1
E-book ISBN: 978-0-7166-2649-7 (EPUB3)

Printed in China by PrintWORKS Global Services, Shenzhen, Guangdong
2nd printing May 2016

Writer: Scott A. Leonard

Staff for World Book, Inc.
Executive Committee
President: Jim O'Rourke
Vice President and Editor in Chief: Paul A. Kobasa
Vice President, Finance: Donald D. Keller
Vice President, Marketing: Jean Lin
Director, International Sales: Kristin Norell
Director, Licensing Sales: Edward Field
Director, Human Resources: Bev Ecker

Editorial
Manager, Annuals/Series Nonfiction: Christine Sullivan
Managing Editor, Annuals/Series Nonfiction:
    Barbara Mayes
Administrative Assistant: Ethel Matthews
Manager, Indexing Services: David Pofelski
Manager, Contracts & Compliance
    (Rights & Permissions): Loranne K. Shields

Manufacturing/Production
Manufacturing Manager: Sandra Johnson
Production/Technology Manager: Anne Fritzinger
Proofreader: Nathalie Strassheim

Graphics and Design
Senior Art Director: Tom Evans
Coordinator, Design Development and Production:
    Brenda Tropinski
Senior Designers: Matthew Carrington,
    Isaiah W. Sheppard, Jr.
Media Researcher: Jeff Heimsath
Manager, Cartographic Services: Wayne K. Pichler
Senior Cartographer: John M. Rejba

Staff for Brown Bear Books Ltd
Managing Editor: Tim Cooke
Editorial Director: Lindsey Lowe
Children's Publisher: Anne O'Daly
Design Manager: Keith Davis
Designer: Mike Davis
Picture Manager: Sophie Mortimer

Picture credits
t=top, c=center, b=bottom, l=left, r=right
4bl, Shutterstock; 5t, Alamy; 6, WORLD BOOK map; 7, EE Topfoto; 8, istockphoto; 10-11, Alamy; 12b, Alamy; 12t, Thinkstock; 13t, Alamy; 13b, Alamy; 14-15, Shutterstock; 15, Alamy; 16-17, Caro/Riedmiller/Topfoto; 18bl, Shutterstock; 18-19t, Alamy; 18br, Alamy; 19b, Topfoto; 20-21, Shutterstock; 21, Alamy; 22, Alamy; 22-23, Shutterstock; 24b, Getty Images; 24tr, Alamy; 25t, SuperStock; 25b, Alamy; 27, Alamy; 29, Alamy; 30b, Topfoto; 30t, Bridgeman Art Library; 31t, Shutterstock; 31b, Thinkstock; 32-33, Alamy; 34, Alamy; 34-35, Alamy; 36b, Shutterstock; 36t, Bridgeman Art Library; 37t, Shutterstock; 37b, Shutterstock; 38-39, Shutterstock; 40-41, Shutterstock; 41, Topfoto; 42b, Thinkstock; 43bl, Shutterstock; 43br, Topfoto; 44-45, Shutterstock; 45, Topfoto; 46-47, Shutterstock; 48t, Alamy; 48b, Topfoto; 49t, Topfoto; 49b, Topfoto; 50-51, Alamy; 52, Topfoto; 52-53t, Topfoto; 52-53b, Corbis; 53, Corbis; 54-55, Thinkstock; 56-57, Shutterstock; 58, Deviant Art; 58-59, Bridgeman Art Library; 59, Alamy; back cover, Shutterstock.

CONTENTS

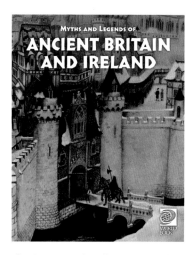

The Green Knight rides into Camelot Castle, the home of King Arthur, to issue his challenge to the Knights of the Round Table, in a 1961 painting by Scottish artist William McLaren.

© ILN/Mary Evans/The Image Works

Note to Readers:
Phonetic pronunciations have been inserted into the myths and legends in this volume to make reading the stories easier and to give the reader some of the flavor of the Celtic cultures the stories represent. See page 64 for a pronunciation key.

The myths and legends retold in this volume are written in a creative way to provide an engaging reading experience and approximate the artistry of the originals. Many of these stories were not written down but were recited by storytellers from generation to generation. Even when some of the stories came to be written down, they likely did not feature phonetic pronunciations for challenging names and words! We hope the inclusion of this material will improve rather than distract from your experience of the stories.

Some of the figures mentioned in the myths and legends in this volume are described on page 60 in the section "Deities and Mythic Characters of Ancient Britain and Ireland." In addition, some unusual words in the text are defined in the Glossary on page 62.

INTRODUCTION

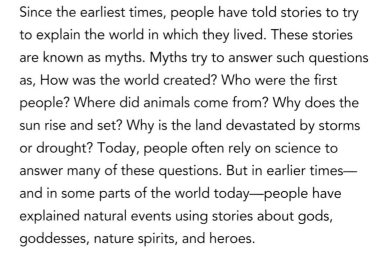

The World of
Oisín, page 42

Since the earliest times, people have told stories to try to explain the world in which they lived. These stories are known as myths. Myths try to answer such questions as, How was the world created? Who were the first people? Where did animals come from? Why does the sun rise and set? Why is the land devastated by storms or drought? Today, people often rely on science to answer many of these questions. But in earlier times—and in some parts of the world today—people have explained natural events using stories about gods, goddesses, nature spirits, and heroes.

Myths are different from folk tales and legends. Folk tales are fictional stories about animals or human beings. Most of these tales are not set in any particular time or place, and they begin and end in a certain way. For example, many English folk tales begin with the phrase "Once upon a time" and end with "They lived happily ever after." Legends are set in the real world, in the present or the historical past. Legends distort the truth, but they are based on real people or events.

Myths, in contrast, typically tell of events that have taken place in the remote past. Unlike legends, myths have also played—and often continue to play—an important role in a society's religious life. Although legends may have religious themes, most are not religious in nature. The people of a society may tell folk tales and legends for amusement, without believing them. But they usually consider their myths sacred and completely true.

Most myths concern *divinities* or *deities* (divine beings). These divinities have powers far greater than those of any human being. At the same time, however, many gods, goddesses, and heroes of mythology have human characteristics. They are guided by such emotions as love and jealousy, and they may experience birth and death. Mythological figures may even look like human beings. Often, the human qualities of the divinities reflect a society's ideals. Good gods and goddesses have the qualities a society admires, and evil ones have the qualities it dislikes. In myths, the actions of these divinities influence the world of humans for better or for worse.

The World of the Celts, page 12

Myths may seem very strange. They sometimes seem to take place in a world that is both like our world and unlike it. Time can go backward and forward, so it is sometimes difficult to tell in what order events happen. People may be dead and alive at the same time.

Myths were originally passed down from generation to generation by word of mouth. Partly for this reason, there are often different versions of the same story. Many myths across cultures share similar themes, such as a battle between good and evil. But the myths of a society generally reflect the landscape, climate, and society in which the storytellers lived.

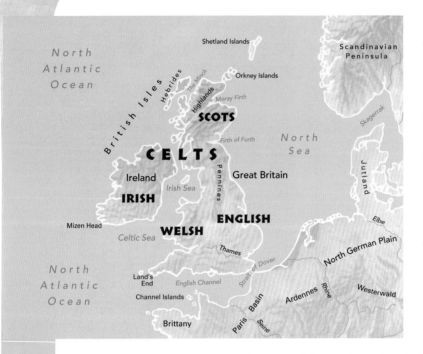

Myths tell people about their distant history. They show people how to behave and find their way. As teaching tools, myths help to prepare children for adulthood.

Myths and Legends of Britain and Ireland

The myths and legends of the British Isles—England, Ireland, Scotland, and Wales—are largely derived from the traditions of the Celts. The Celts were a diverse group of ancient peoples who shared a common language, religion, and culture. They were one of the most important ancient peoples of Europe. They emerged in Austria in the center of that continent and eventually spread across much of it. Their culture influenced most of northern and western Europe during the Iron Age, beginning about 700 B.C.

Much of our information on Celtic mythology concerns mythical characters and events in Ireland. During the Middle Ages, from about the A.D. 400's through the 1400's, Irish monks preserved many ancient Celtic myths in several collections of manuscripts.

The British Isles are made up of Great Britain, including England, Scotland, and Wales; Ireland, made up of Northern Ireland and the country of Ireland; the Isle of Man; the Hebrides; the Orkney Islands; the Shetland Islands; and about 5,500 small islands and islets. The Romans occupied England from 55 B.C. to the early 400's, but most of Wales, Scotland, and Ireland remained home to Celtic peoples.

The Celtic dominance of central Europe brought them into conflict with the growing Roman Empire. The two opponents fought many battles, but the Romans eventually drove the Celts to the very edges of their empire. By the first century A.D., the Celts survived only in Ireland, Wales, Scotland, and Brittany in northern France. The Irish Celts remembered the successive waves of settlers who moved to Ireland in myths that recall a series of invasions by legendary peoples.

The Celts in Britain and Ireland began to convert to Christianity before the A.D. 400's. After the fall of the Roman Empire, the Celts came under the influence of Germanic peoples of northern Europe, though there was a flowering of Celtic culture from the 500's to 700's. Later, Celtic themes emerged in stories of the famous English ruler, King Arthur. The tales of Arthur and the knights of the Round Table also reflected such Christian themes as the quest for the Holy Grail.

The World of King
Arthur, page 48

Although many of the stories in this book appear simple at first glance, they are layered with meaning. Each retelling of the story reveals a new meaning. Understanding these myths is necessary for any kind of understanding of the societies that created them. By studying myths, we can learn how different societies have answered basic questions about the world and the individual's place in it.

8

THE BIRTH OF LUGH

The Irish Celts told this story to explain the birth of one of their great heroes, a supernaturally gifted king named Lugh, who helped to bring together warring dynasties and found the Irish race.

Balor (BAH lor), the Great Smiter, was the king of a race of hideously ugly giants called the Fomorians (foh MAHR ee uhnz). In the middle of Balor's forehead was a single poisonous eye that he covered with seven woolen blankets.

When Balor removed the top blanket, the ferns and water-loving plants on Earth withered. As he removed each additional blanket, the land became drier and hotter. Whenever Balor removed all seven blankets, everything he saw turned to tinder and burst into flame. In battle, none could withstand the Great Smiter once his terrible eye was uncovered.

But Balor lived in fear. For Druids (DROO ihdz), learned people who could see the future, had predicted that a child born of his daughter, Ethniu (EHN yuh), would one day kill him. To prevent this, Balor locked Ethniu in a tower on Tory Island, ordering 12 women to keep her from ever meeting a man. But neither Balor nor the 12 watching women could guard Ethniu's mind. And so a handsome man sometimes appeared in her dreams.

On the mainland lived three brothers— Cian (KEE ahn), Samthainn (SOH ehn), and Goibniu (GOY nee oo) the Smith, a worker of metal. Cian, lord of his clan, owned Gloss Gavlen (glas gav lehn), a white cow with green spots that produced milk and calves in astonishing abundance. The cow had made the clan rich, and other clans wanted to steal her. So the brothers were forced to escort Gloss Gavlen from shed to pasture, guarding her constantly.

One day, Cian left the miraculous cow in Samthainn's care while he went to Goibniu's forge. As Samthainn kept watch, Balor, in the form of a red-haired boy, approached him.

"Do you know, sir," the disguised Balor said to Samthainn, "that your brothers plot against you?"

"How so?" asked Samthainn, alarmed. "Even now Cian and Goibniu have taken iron from your forge to make Cian a great sword that he will use to kill you," the red-haired boy replied.

"Stay here, boy, while I look into this," said Samthainn. "Make sure no harm comes to that cow yonder." As soon as Samthainn was out of sight, Balor resumed his form, led Gloss Gavlen to his boat, and sailed to Tory Island.

When Cian saw Samthainn approaching the forge, he knew Gloss Gavlen was lost. He watched helplessly as Balor and the cow sailed away.

Cian searched for a way to retrieve his prized cow, eventually approaching Birog (BIHR ohg), a mountain fairy. "None can withstand Balor's Evil Eye," said Birog. "Gloss Gavlen cannot be retrieved while Balor lives."

"Then how do I kill him?" asked Cian. "You cannot, brave Cian," replied the fairy. "Another will perform that task."

Then, summoning a mighty wind, Birog transported Cian to Tory Island. Ethniu recognized the young lord as the man in her dreams and soon fell in love with him. In time, she gave birth to triplets.

Balor, enraged that imprisoning his daughter had failed to prevent her from giving birth to children, ordered the three boys placed in a sack and thrown into the sea. But the sack broke as it entered the water, and the babies floated free. Sadly, two of the boys drowned. However, Birog, who had been watching for such a chance, rescued the surviving baby and bore him to his father, Cian, who named him Lugh (loo).

Fearing for the boy's safety, Cian sent Lugh to the goddess Taillte (tahl tuh) of the Great Plain. Protected and loved, Lugh was blessed with a quiet life— for a time.

The World of
THE CELTS

The Celts (kehlts) were a diverse group of ancient inhabitants of Europe. The name has also traditionally been used for the peoples of Iron Age Britain and Ireland. At its greatest, Celtic culture extended from present-day Portugal to the Balkans, and from Austria to the southern coast of France. In continental Europe, Celts spread by migration to new areas. Celtic culture arrived in Britain and Ireland sometime after 500 B.C. In these areas, however, Celtic culture spread through contact and trade with continental Celts rather than by migration. A number of modern languages, including Irish, Scottish Gaelic, Manx Gaelic, Welsh, and Cornish, come from the Celtic language.

The village of Hallstatt, near Salzburg, Austria, (bottom in photo) has produced the earliest evidence of Celtic culture. Archaeologists working there have discovered nearly 2,000 Celtic burials dating from about 700 to 500 B.C.

A man and a woman in Celtic dress cook a meal at a reconstructed Iron Age village at Navan Centre & Fort, an interpretive center near the city of Armagh (ahr MAH), in Northern Ireland.

THE IRON AGE

The Iron Age is the period in history when the use of iron became widespread. It followed the Bronze Age, which followed the Stone Age. People in certain areas had begun to *smelt* (melt) iron ore and use the iron for tools by about 3500 B.C., during the Bronze Age. Iron's chief advantage was its cheapness—because iron ore is found everywhere—and its strength. Workers did not have to *alloy* (combine) iron with other metals to form an effective tool or weapon. The Celts were among the first peoples in Europe to work with iron.

Ethniu (EHN yuh), the daughter of Balor (BAH lohr), meets the man in her dreams, Cian (KEE ahn), in an illustration from 1905.

Druids (DROO ihdz) cut mistletoe in the forest for use as charms for Celtic people while being watched by Roman soldiers. Druids were the learned, priestly class among the Celts. After conquering much of Britain in the A.D. 80's, the Romans tried to eliminate Druidism, the religion of the Celts. This religion was *polytheistic*—that is, it involved the worship of hundreds of male and female deities. Celtic rituals often took place in groves or near pools, wells, or springs considered to be sacred to one or more of these deities. The Celts believed in a life after death and in another world, sometimes called Tir na nOg (teer na nohg), the Land of Forever-Young.

LUGH Defeats Balor

Lugh might have grown up quietly, but he was destined to play a key role in history. Meanwhile, his grandfather, Balor the Great Smiter, never forgot the prophecy that Lugh would destroy him.

When he became an adult, Lugh (loo) wanted to join his father's people, the magical Tuatha De Danann (too AH hah day dah NAHN), the People of the Goddess Danu (DAHN oo). When he arrived at the gates of Tara, the home of the Tuatha De Danann, Lugh said, "I am Lugh, son of Cian (KEE ahn) and Ethniu (EHN yuh), grandson of Balor (BAH lohr). Tell King Nuada (noo uh duh) I wish to join his house." "None may enter Tara unless they have a unique skill," replied the gatekeeper.

"I am a carpenter," declared Lugh. "We have a carpenter," replied the gate-keeper. "I am a smith," Lugh answered. "We also have a smith," replied the gate-keeper." This went on for some time. Lugh told the gatekeeper that he was a champion, a warrior, a harpist, a bard, a physician, and so on.

The gatekeeper replied that Tara already possessed someone skilled in each of these areas. "Do you have anyone skilled in all of these areas? If so, I will trouble you no more," said Lugh.

The gatekeeper reported to King Nuada that a man at the gates claimed to be Samildanach (SAV ihl dah nahk), the Master of All Arts. The king replied, "Set up a chessboard and send for the best players!" Lugh played and defeated the best players in Tara. Seeing this, King Nuada declared, "Truly he is Samildanach! Allow him entry."

Now, at this time, the Tuatha De Danann were ruled harshly by the hideously ugly Fomorians (foh MAHR ee uhnz). One day, Lugh asked the king,

"Why do you live as Fomor slaves?"
"They are too many and too mighty,"
said King Nuada. "Better to die fighting
for freedom than to live as slaves!"
Lugh declared.

For a year, Lugh, King Nuada, and the
Tuatha De Danann's four other leaders—
the chief Druid Dagda (DOY duh), the
physician Diancecht (DY an keht), the
champion Ogma (Ug m), and Goibniu
(GOY nee oo) the Smith—secretly
discussed how they might free their
people. They decided that to prevent the
Fomorians from suspecting a revolution
was afoot, they would wait three years
before acting. In the meantime, Lugh
sought the aid of Manannán mac Lir
(MAN an ahn mahk lihr), God of the Sea.

At the appointed time, Lugh returned,
shining like a second sun and wearing
Manannán's impenetrable armor. He
rode Embarr (ehm bahr), the horse that
galloped over land and sea, and wielded
Answerer, a sword that rendered the
bravest warriors cowards and made cuts
from which none recovered.

Now Balor was troubled to hear that his
grandson led a great army. For years, the
Smiter had dreaded the prophecy that
Lugh would liberate the Tuatha De
Danann and cause Balor's death. So Balor
plotted with Bres (brehs) the Beautiful,
the exiled king of the Tuatha De Danann.
Together, they determined to bring war
against King Nuada and destroy the
threat to Balor's safety once and for all.

But King Nuada and the Tuatha De
Danann acted first. The king's cup-
bearers arranged it so the lakes and
wells gave no water to the Fomor but
provided Nuada's soldiers all they could
drink. The Druids rained fire and disease

on the Fomor army. Goibniu the Smith made swords and spearheads that would never miss their mark. Cairbre (KAR bihr eh), the bard, sang a poem about the Fomor to make them lose heart. The physician Diancecht promised to plunge the wounded and dead Tuatha De Danann warriors into a magical well each night. By morning, the warriors would be ready to fight again.

King Nuada thought Lugh too valuable to risk in battle, so he ordered nine champions to hold him behind the lines. The fighting was fierce. Although the wounds of the Tuatha De Danann were healed each night and their dead brought back to life, and although their swords and spears always found their marks, still they could not win a decisive victory. Days passed, and the ground became slick with blood.

In a last desperate effort, Balor entered the fighting. Hearing this, Lugh escaped his guard and raced to the front lines. But he was too late. Balor killed King Nuada with a single sword-stroke.

Lugh, seeing his dead king, challenged Balor. "Help me lift my eyelid," roared the Great Smiter to his followers, "so I may destroy Lugh!" But just as Balor's Evil Eye was opening, Lugh fired a stone from his sling with such force that the Eye burst through the back of Balor's head, and he was killed.

Hundreds of Fomorian soldiers fell when they came under the sight of the dying Eye. After Lugh beheaded Balor, the Smiter's army fled. The few surviving Fomorians boarded their boats and never returned to Ireland.

The World of
LUGH AND BALOR

The Celts (kehlts) divided what is now Ireland into about 150 communities called *tuatha* (TOO ah). Each tuatha was ruled by a king. Celtic kings lived in houses fortified by banks of earth, or in *crannogs*, houses built on artificial islands in lakes, like this reconstructed crannog in County Clare, in the Republic of Ireland (right). Sometimes a group of kings recognized one of their number as an *overking*. In the same way, a number of overkings formed a kind of federation under the king of one of the country's five provinces. Ireland's original provinces, sometimes called the *five fifths of Ireland*, were probably Ulster (UHL stuhr), in what is now Northern Ireland; and Leinster (LAYN stuhr), Munster (MUHN stuhr), Connacht (KON naht), and Meath (meed), in what is now the Republic of Ireland.

The Legananny Dolmen (lehg ahn anh ee DOL muhn) in Northern Ireland is an impressive example of these Celtic stone monuments built over graves or tombs.

Celtic reenactors fight using axes and a large wooden shield. In Celtic society, the power of a king was usually based on his ability on the battlefield.

TUATHA DE DANANN

Lugh (loo) and the Tuatha De Danann (too AH hah day dah NAHN) are part of the mythological *cycle* (series of related stories), one of the main sources of Irish Celtic mythology. The cycle describes the early settlement of what is now Ireland through a series of invasions by supernatural races. The most important race was the Tuatha De Danann, or People of the Goddess Danu (DAHN oo). The Tuatha used their magic powers to defeat two other races, the Firbolgs (FEER buhl uhgz) and the Fomorians (foh MAHR ee uhnz). The Tuatha De Danann were in turn defeated by the Sons of Mil, also called the Milesians (my LEE zhuhnz), a Celtic group from the northwestern Iberian Peninsula. The Milesians drove the Tuatha De Danann underground into hills called *sídhe* (shee).

Massive stone walls surround a hillfort named Grianán of Aileach (gree nahn of ee lee) in the Republic of Ireland. The walls date from the A.D. 500's or 600's, though people probably lived at the site much earlier. The hillfort served as the seat of a Celtic kingdom for some 600 years. Destroyed by another Irish king in 1101, Grianán of Aileach was restored in the 1870's. The hillfort has traditionally been linked to the Tuatha De Danann.

CUCHULAINN'S

The story of Cuchulainn (koo KUHL ihn) describes the origins of one of the great heroes of Irish myth, who was said to be destined to live a short life but whose name would live on forever.

Cuchulainn (koo KUHL ihn) was known as Sétanta (SHAY dan duh) when he was a boy. When Sétanta was only five, he set off for the city of Emain Macha (EH vin MA ka) because he heard that 150 boys, led by Prince Folloman (FOHL uh vuhn), were playing there. Custom demanded that anyone who wanted to join the boy-troop should first win from them a pledge of protection. But little Sétanta was ignorant of the custom and instead rushed onto the field, stole the boys' ball, and made a brilliant goal.

The boys were furious and began throwing bats, balls, and spears at Sétanta, intending to kill him. But the little boy deflected every missile with his toy staff. As Sétanta grew angrier and angrier, his appearance changed to that of a Cyclops with a halo of fire about his head and a gaping mouth stretching from ear to ear. He flattened 50 boys before Conchobar

mac Nessa (KON cho var mak nessa), king of Emain Macha, calmed him.

"Didn't you know," asked the king, "that custom requires all newcomers to ask the boy-troop for protection?" "I did not," Sétanta replied. "Well then, boys," Conchobar ordered, "forgive this over-sight and grant this lad your protection."

The boys obeyed, but no sooner had play resumed than Sétanta again began smashing the older boys to the ground. "What is this?!" demanded Conchobar. "I will not ease up until each of these boys comes under MY protection!" Sétanta declared. Seeing that Sétanta could easily overpower any of the older boys, Conchobar agreed, and, thus, a child became the protector of boys twice his age.

YOUTH

Later that year, King Conchobar attended a feast hosted by Culann (KOO lihn) the Smith. Passing by the grassy common ground in the center of town, King Conchobar was astonished to see the boys playing a game of hole ball in which 150 of the boys defended their goal against only Sétanta. Try as the older boys might to put one of their 150 balls into the hole on Sétanta's end of the field, the younger boy caught them all. And try as they might to defend their goal, the younger boy succeeded in getting his ball into their hole.

"I want that boy to join us at Culann's feast," said King Conchobar. But headstrong Sétanta refused to come right away. "I'll catch up with you once the boys have had enough play," he said. The king's company rode on, and soon Conchobar forgot all about Sétanta.

When the royal company arrived at Culann's fortress, the Smith greeted them with due ceremony. "Are others coming?" asked Culann. "I'm about to release my bloodhound to guard the property. He is an astonishing beast with the strength of hundreds. He recognizes only me and will tear to pieces any who approach." "Our company is complete," replied Conchobar.

After Sétanta finished play, he hurried down the road to join the king. When he reached Culann's yard, the fierce hound sprang at him. Sétanta's only defense was a ball, which he threw into the mouth of the dog with such force that it carried the beast's guts out through its rear end. Sétanta then seized the animal by the forelegs and bashed him to pieces against a rock.

Hearing the commotion, the feasters rushed into the yard only to discover Sétanta standing unhurt with the remains of the dog. They were amazed—but Culann was furious. "You have cost me a friend and my livelihood, boy!" he declared. "Not only did the dog guard my house at night, he guarded my flocks by day, making me prosperous."

"Don't be angry, Master Culann!" replied Sétanta. "I will be your hound until a pup from the bloodhound's line can be trained to replace him." The men murmured their approval at this resolution to an embarrassing breach of hospitality. From that day, Sétanta was called Cuchulainn, the Hound of Culann.

Cuchulainn (koo KUHL ihn) was said to be the son of the god Lugh (loo) and Deichtine (DEHK tuhr ah), the sister of Conchobar mac Nessa (KON cho var mak nessa). Like the Greek hero Achilles (uh KIHL eez), Cuchulainn chooses a short, adventurous life and everlasting fame over a long, quiet life and obscurity. Cuchulainn inspired both jealousy and terror in others. In part, this was because he went into "battle frenzy," a state that warped his features into those of a monster that destroyed friend and foe alike. One of his many memorable battles was against Ferdiad (fur dee ah), his best friend. After fighting for three days, Cuchulainn killed Ferdiad at a *ford* (river crossing) (right).

The enlarged heads on a Celtic (KEHL tihk) statue of a two-faced god reflect the spiritual significance of the god among the Celts (kehlts). They saw the head as the seat of the soul and the center of a man's power. When a warrior was killed in battle, his enemy usually beheaded him and took away the head as a sign that the victor had absorbed the power of his former enemy.

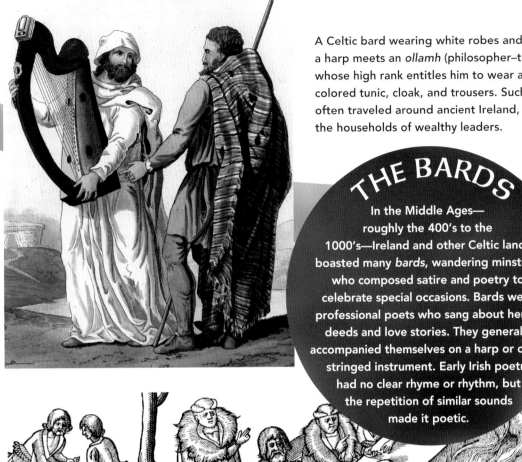

A Celtic bard wearing white robes and carrying a harp meets an *ollamh* (philosopher–teacher), whose high rank entitles him to wear a brightly colored tunic, cloak, and trousers. Such men often traveled around ancient Ireland, visiting the households of wealthy leaders.

THE BARDS

In the Middle Ages— roughly the 400's to the 1000's—Ireland and other Celtic lands boasted many *bards*, wandering minstrels who composed satire and poetry to celebrate special occasions. Bards were professional poets who sang about heroic deeds and love stories. They generally accompanied themselves on a harp or other stringed instrument. Early Irish poetry had no clear rhyme or rhythm, but the repetition of similar sounds made it poetic.

A bard sings to the accompaniment of a harp to entertain an Irish chieftain during a meal. Early Irish culture was passed on by word of mouth. Professional poets called the *filid* (FEE leed) put early Ireland's customs, history, and laws into verse, which made long lists of facts easier to recall. In the 1500's, there was a gradual decline in support of the filid, which grew worse after the conquest of Ireland by England and the arrival in Ireland of greater numbers of English settlers. The defeat of the Irish chieftains early in the 1600's furthered the decline. Irish storytellers called *seanchaithe* (SHEN uh kith ee) continue to preserve the oral tradition of their people in modern times.

THE CATTLE RAID

When the bickering of King Ailill and Queen Maeve brought war between the provinces of Connacht and Ulster, Cuchulainn led the Ulster forces into battle—and came face to face with his old companion, Fergus.

The bickering of King Ailill (AL yil) and Queen Maeve (mayv) of the province of Connacht (KON naht) led to a war with the people of the province of Ulster (UHL stuhr).

"Like all women," said Ailill, "you are well off because you married a rich and powerful man." "Not so!" spat Maeve. "Before we met, I was richer than my father and brothers—and better in battle than them. Marrying me was the making of you!"

The queen and king had their servants bring out their precious possessions to compare their wealth. Maeve's wealth equaled Ailill's own in every respect but one. He possessed the bull Finnbennach (FIHN vehn ahk), which had been born of Maeve's herd but had refused to remain in a woman's keeping. So Maeve asked Darè (DAH ruh), who owned the Brown Bull of Cuailnge (kell nee)—the king of bulls—if she could borrow his bull for a year so it might sire a bull equal to Finnbennach. But Darè, a man of Ulster, refused.

Maeve decided to take the Brown Bull by force. She mustered four armies at Cruachain (CREW ach uhn), her seat of power. She consulted her Druid (DROO ihd), seeking an omen. The seer spoke: "I see a beautiful youth, Cuchulainn (koo KUHL ihn), the Hound of Culann (KOO lihn). In battle, he takes the form of a dragon. He will destroy your armies."

Nevertheless, Maeve gave marching orders. Fergus (FEHR guhs), formerly a man of Ulster and companion of Cuchulainn, led her host. Cuchulainn met Maeve's army head-on and alone.

Battle frenzy took hold of him, and his appearance changed. Like an unreasoning fiend, Cuchulainn fell on the enemy. He killed hundreds of Maeve's warriors a day, stacking their corpses to form walls.

Soon there was turmoil in Maeve's army. None dared face Cuchulainn. Exasperated, Maeve sent Fergus to face the Hound in single combat. It grieved Fergus to fight his childhood friend. But the next morning, he met Cuchulainn.

"Have you come to fight me, friend?" asked Cuchulainn. But Fergus suggested a plan. "Give way before me this day, and I will give way before you on a day when you are wounded and bloody."

And so it was agreed. Cuchulainn fled as though terrified before Fergus. Seeing their champion seemingly defeated, the army from Ulster that had arrived to support Cuchulainn retreated as well. And so Maeve's armies seemed to win the battle.

But in the following days, when Maeve's greatest champions came against Cuchulainn, the mighty hero took their heads. Even Ferdiad (fur dee ah), Maeve's son, fell before the Hound's sword-stroke, though the battle lasted for three days.

After a time, Cuchulainn, exhausted from his wounds, returned to camp. The battle turned against the Ulstermen. Bloodlust then took Fergus. "I will pull heads from shoulders and scatter the limbs of the Ulstermen today!"

So saying, he lifted Hardblade, his sword, and fell upon the Ulster host. Cuchulainn, hearing that Fergus was leading the charge and that the dead of Ulster would soon surpass the living, forgot his wounds. He ran to the battlefront so quickly he forgot his sword. So he wielded his chariot like a club, smashing Maeve's soldiers.

When at last Cuchulainn faced Fergus, both men were covered in the gore of the slain. "Did you not vow to run before me, Fergus, on a day when I was wounded and covered in blood?" demanded Cuchulainn.

"I will keep my oath," replied Fergus, before turning to flee. Then Maeve's host lost heart and fled with him. Cuchulainn cornered Queen Maeve but considered it dishonorable to kill a woman. Instead, he guarded her and her followers until they crossed the border back to Cruachain.

The World of
QUEEN MAEVE AND CUCHULAINN

Cruachain (CREW ach uhn) was the mythical seat of power of King Ailill (AL yil) and Queen Maeve (mayv). Evil creatures were said to emerge from Oweynagat (o WEAN a ga), the hill where Cruachain stood, including a flock of red birds, whose breath withered plants, and Ellen Trechen, a three-headed beast. An archaeological site named Cruachain, near Tulsk in the Republic of Ireland, is identified with the traditional capital of the Connacht (KON naht), rivals of the Ulstermen in myth.

Cuchulainn (koo KUHL ihn) traps Queen Maeve in a wood after defeating Fergus (FEHR guhs), her champion. Believing it was dishonorable to kill a woman, Cuchulainn escorted the queen back to her kingdom.

Many earth mounds and stones around Ireland are linked with the *aes sidhe,* who are said to live there.

IRISH FAIRIES

The Irish called fairies *aes sidhe* (EYE shee). The earth mounds dotting the Irish landscape are called *sidhe,* and fairies were thought to live beneath them. Today, fairies are imagined as cute winged creatures. Before the 1700's, however, a fairy might be any supernatural creature (except a monster or demon). In folklore and myth, they were often imagined as glowing humanlike creatures living in a world parallel to our own. They could be treacherous, and tales depict them as doing great mischief.

The lush grass and damp climate of Ireland are ideal for raising cattle.

After reading "The Cattle Raid of Cuailnge," it might be easy to think that the early Irish relied for food almost entirely on their livestock. But studies of ancient pollen have proved that grain (below)—and therefore farming—was central to the diet and economy of Ireland beginning around A.D. 200. However, cattle were important enough that most of Ireland's forests were cleared for grazing land. Cattle raids, like the one in this story, may well have been the cause of large-scale skirmishes between landowners.

FINN MACCOOL
and the Salmon of Knowledge

The story of the Salmon of Knowledge explains the great wisdom attributed to the hero Finn MacCool and reflects the importance the Celts placed on intelligence as well as physical strength and courage.

Finn MacCool was just a baby when his father was murdered. To protect Finn from the assassins, his Druid (DROO ihd) aunts took him to a forested hideout, where they raised him under the name Deimne (DAY nee). His father's killers found Finn's hiding place, so the boy wandered the countryside, never stopping for long. When at last he met the poet Finegas (FIN ay gas), he found a home. Kind and patient, Finegas was a gifted teacher. Like all intelligent children, Finn was bursting with questions, and Finegas never tired of answering them.

"Why do you live by the River Boyne?" asked Finn. "Because a poem is a revelation revealed only near the sound of running water," Finegas answered.

"So why this river and not another?" Finn pressed. "Because I received a prophecy declaring I would catch the Salmon of Knowledge if I lived by Boyne Water." "What then?" asked Finn. "Then I would have All Knowledge," Finegas said.

"How does the salmon get knowledge into its flesh?" asked Finn. "A sacred hazel bush hangs over a hidden pool," replied Finegas. "The hazel bush drops its nuts, the Nuts of Knowledge, into the water, and the salmon eats them."

"What are we waiting for?!" cried Finn. "Why not follow the river and find these nuts ourselves?" "Magic hides the hazel. Only by eating the Salmon of Knowledge can one learn the location of the sacred bush," Finegas told his pupil.

And so Finn passed days, months, and years in Finegas's company. His body grew strong, and so did his mind. Finn learned much lore and how to ask good questions and arrive at good answers.

One day, Finn saw Finegas approaching with a willow basket. His teacher had an odd look on his face. "Is all well, master?" asked Finn. "Look in the basket," said Finegas.

"It's a lovely salmon! We will feast tonight!" Finn said happily. "It's the

Salmon of Knowledge, boy," exlaimed Finegas.

"Oh, master, please eat it so you may possess all knowledge!" Finn urged. "Will you cook it for me, Finn?" asked Finegas. "I need to rest awhile. Mind you, don't eat my fish." "I will not!" declared Finn.

Soon the aroma of roasting salmon filled the air. When Finegas returned, he looked stern. "Have you eaten any of my fish?" "Of course not!" replied Finn. "Not even a morsel?" asked Finegas.

"Well, as the fish cooked," admitted Finn, "I saw a blister rising on its skin. When I pushed it down, I burned my thumb and sucked it to make it feel better. If your salmon tastes as good as my thumb, you will be happy!"

Finegas's stern look turned to sorrow. "I'm afraid I haven't told you the truth, boy—not all of it," he said.

"Omitting part of the truth is not a very great lie, master," said Finn. "It must not grow greater!" replied Finegas. "The prophecy that I would catch the Salmon of Knowledge also said that I would not eat of it. That honor would belong to the son of Uail (ool)—and he was your father, wasn't he, boy?"

"Yes, sir. But at least share the fish with me." "No!" said Finegas. "I will praise the gods that their word has been fulfilled and that I have played my part." From that day, Finn had only to put his thumb in his mouth when he was puzzled to discover the solution to a problem.

The World of **FINN MACCOOL**

Finn MacCool and his warrior band, the Fianna (FEE uh nuh), appear in the Fionn (FEE ahn) cycle, a series of stories that is one of the four main sources of Irish Celtic (KEHL tihk) mythology. The Fianna were small war bands in Irish and Scottish myths that roamed the land. In myths, they were sometimes housed and fed by nobles, for whom they enforced order or waged war. There seems to be some link between the Fianna of myth and bands of landless youth who, in medieval times, had to live by hunting, fishing, and selling or exchanging the skins of animals they hunted for other necessities.

↑
As a boy living in the woods, Finn MacCool sees a horse and feels sad that he does not have a tail to brush the flies away, according to one myth about the Celtic hero.

The salmon featured in the myth of Finn MacCool is one of a number of the fish that appear in Celtic myths. The salmon was associated mainly with wisdom and the ability to see the future. Salmon were often said to live in sacred wells.

Finn's partner, Sabdh (sive), was transformed into a deer by a Druid (DROO ihd) whose advances she rejected.

CELTIC GIANTS

The ancient Celts believed in giants, enormous humanlike creatures. They are usually depicted in myths as brutal, violent, and stupid. The ancient Celts thought that giants must have existed because it seemed impossible that such structures as Stonehenge could have been built by human hands. In addition, notable landforms, including the Giant's Causeway in Ireland and various islands off Britain's coast, seemed to have been constructed rather than formed through natural processes.

The Giant's Causeway is an unusual formation of volcanic rock columns along the north coast of Northern Ireland. It gets its name from an old legend that the causeway was built by Finn MacCool to bridge the channel from Ireland to Scotland so that giants could pass over it. The causeway is formed of about 40,000 separate columns, quite close together. Some pillars are up to 20 feet (6 meters) high. They are from 15 to 20 inches (38 to 51 centimeters) in diameter. Geologists believe the causeway resulted from the contraction, or shrinking, of a lava flow.

OISÍN
in the Land of Forever-Young

This story helped to explain how traditional tales of fairies and the supernatural survived Ireland's conversion to Christianity, as represented by Saint Patrick, who appears at the end of the tale.

Tir na nOg (teer na nohg) lies under the sea. Some call it the Land of Forever-Young, for none age there. In elder days, it was the custom in Tir na nOg to choose a king through a contest. A chair was placed on a hill near the palace, and every man in the realm raced to the top of the hill. The first to sit on the chair was king for seven years.

Manannán mac Lir (MAN an ahn mahk lihr), the Sea God, had repeatedly won the contest and so had been king for many years. But he feared the day another would replace him. Consulting with his Druid (DROO ihd) priest, Manannán mac Lir learned that he would hold the throne forever, unless he had a son-in-law. His daughter, Niahm (nee ihv), was more beautiful than any other woman, and many sought her hand. To prevent her marrying, Manannán cast a spell, giving his daughter a pig's head.

"Must I always remain like this?" Niamh asked the Druid. He consoled her by saying, "If you go to Ireland and marry one of the sons of Finn MacCool, you will become as you were."

Niamh mounted Embarr (ehm bahr), the steed that gallops equally well over water and land, and set off for Ireland. She learned that Finn MacCool and the other Fianna (FEE uh nuh) lived in Knock an Ar.

In the woods outside Finn's fort, Niamh followed some hunters. She approached the most successful hunter. "Forgive my boldness," said the man, "but I've never seen a woman with a pig's head before."

"I was cursed to wear this face unless I marry a son of Finn MacCool," Niamh replied.

"I am Oisín (uhsh EEN), Finn's son. And I daresay you will not wear that pig's head much longer." "You will have me as wife, then?" Niamh asked. "That is well, but I come from Tir na nOg, and my time in your world is brief. To have me, you must come back with me to fairyland." "Lead on, wife!" said Oisín.

Oisín followed Niamh to the Land of Forever-Young. Manannán mac Lir was so delighted that his daughter had returned that he forgot about the prophecy and welcomed Oisín as his son-in-law.

Not long after, Oisín joined the other men in the competition for kingship. When the horn sounded, all surged forward; but halfway up the hill, they stopped. Oisín was already sitting on the throne! Manannán gave up his throne, and no one challenged Oisín after that.

Finn's son ruled for some time, but he began to be homesick. "I wish to see my father and the Fianna at least one more time," Oisín said to Niamh. "Time works differently in Tir na nOg than it does in Ireland," she warned him. "You've been here a few short years, but centuries have passed over your homeland."

Oisín heard her words but had to see for himself. "As you wish," said Niamh. "My horse Embarr will bear you to Ireland. But, beware! If you touch the soil, you will become exceedingly old, and Embarr will return without you." "Don't worry! I have every reason to return," said Oisín. "But I must see my homeland one last time."

It was as Niamh had said. Nothing looked familiar. Oisín discovered that Finn and the Fianna had perished centuries before and existed now only in legend. In a field, he saw cattle grazing next to a large stone. Leaning down from Embarr, Oisín turned the stone over and saw Borabu (BOHR uh boo), the Fianna's battle-horn. If only he could sound it, the remnants of his people might come! But as he leaned over to collect the horn, he lost his balance and fell to the ground. In an instant, Embarr galloped away, and Oisín became an extremely old man.

A cattle herder who was nearby ran to tell Saint Patrick what he had seen. The venerable priest gave the aged Oisín a bed, asking him many questions about the old days. With the last of his strength, Oisín told Patrick about the exploits of the Fianna. And thus these tales survive to our own time.

The World of
OISÍN

Oisín's (uhsh EENS) journey to Tir na nOg (teer na nohg) represents a literary *genre* (form) known as *echtra*, which follows a hero as he visits or explores the Otherworld. The hero usually is invited on this journey by what he thinks is a woman or a warrior but who turns out to be Manannán mac Lir (MAN an ahn mahk lihr) or a fairy or a Tuatha De Danann (too AH hah day dah NAHN). In some stories, the hero stays in the Otherworld forever. In other stories, he returns to his people, carrying special knowledge or useful gifts.

Oisín conjures the spirits of Celtic heroes with his ➡ singing, in a painting from the 1800's.

OISÍN

Oisín, whose name means *young deer*, is credited with authoring the Fionn (FEE ahn) cycle. Oisín was said to be the son of Finn MacCool by Sabdh (sive), who had been transformed by a Druid (DROO ihd) into a deer. Finn found her while hunting and took her into his house, where she became a woman again. But after some time together, she changed back into a deer and disappeared. Seven years later, Finn found a boy in the woods (Oisín) and claimed him as his son. Oisín fought alongside his father and had several adventures of his own.

A highly ornamented "P" is one of the glories of the *Book of Kells,* an *illuminated* (decorated) manuscript of the four Gospels and related material in Latin. It was produced between the mid-700's and early 800's, perhaps in the monastery at Kells in Ireland.

Saint Patrick probably had little to do with the preservation of pre-Christian Irish literature. But Irish monasteries were important centers of learning in post-Roman Europe, and their resident scholars played a major role in preserving that literature. But the monks also edited these materials. Gods like Lugh (loo) and Manannán, for example, were transformed into ancient kings. In addition, certain supernatural elements were eliminated to help the Catholic Church stamp out the belief in many deities and spirits.

ST. PATRICK

Saint Patrick is the patron saint of Ireland. Although he was not the first Christian missionary to Ireland, Patrick was chiefly responsible for converting the Irish to Christianity. Patrick was born in Britain to a wealthy Christian father in about A.D. 389. When Patrick was 16 years old, pirates kidnapped him during a raid and sold him as a slave in Ireland. He served as a shepherd for an Irish chieftain in Ulster (UHL stuhr), in what is now Northern Ireland. During his captivity, Patrick took a great interest in religion and dedicated himself to prayer. After six years of slavery, he escaped and returned to Britain.

Patrick developed a great desire to convert the Irish to Christianity. To prepare for this task, Patrick prayed and studied at a monastery off the coast of France. He later went to Auxerre (oh SAIR), France, to study religion. In 431, Palladius (pah LAY dee uhs), the first missionary bishop to Ireland, died. Pope Celestine (SEHL uh styn) I then sent Patrick to Ireland. Patrick began his work in northern and western Ireland, where Christianity had never been preached. Winning the trust and friendship of several tribal leaders, Patrick made many converts. He is considered to have established more than 300 churches and baptized more than 120,000 people. Until his death in 461, Patrick preached and ministered throughout Ireland.

A Celtic cross has a circle, or concentric circles, at the joint of the two bars. The circle touches all four projecting arms.

43

SIR GAWAIN AND THE

In this story about one of the knights of the Round Table, a giant represents pagan religions common in Britain before the arrival of Christianity.

One New Year's Eve, King Arthur, Queen Guenevere (GWEHN uh vihr), and the knights of the Round Table were feasting in Camelot (KAM uh lot) when a giant man arrived. He was strong, handsome—and green. His skin was green; his clothes were green; his weapons were green. He had a big green beard and long, green hair. He even rode a green horse with a green saddle. The Green Knight wore no armor but carried a holly branch in one hand and an ax in the other.

Arthur welcomed the newcomer, who asked the king for a gift. The Green Knight challenged anyone there to strike off his head with his mighty ax. In return, the Green Knight would be allowed to try to chop off the challenger's head on the next New Year's Eve. The room went quiet. Then Arthur's nephew Gawain (guh WAYN) agreed to take up the challenge.

The Green Knight bowed his neck. Gawain lifted his great sword and struck his head off. Blood burst from the wound, but the Green Knight did not fall. He simply lifted his head from the floor and told Gawain he would be at the Green Chapel in the woods in a year. Then, carrying his head, the giant left Camelot.

Ten months later, Gawain set off with a heavy heart to find the Green Chapel and meet his doom. He rode deep into Wales before, on Christmas Eve, he came upon a castle. The lord of the castle, Sir Bertilak, invited Gawain to stay for Christmas. Bertilak said that he himself would be out hunting each day. But he said that his wife would entertain Gawain while he was gone.

The two men would meet again in the evening and exchange whatever they had gained during the day.

Each day for three days, Bertilak went out hunting, leaving Gawain at home. On the first and second days, Bertilak's wife visited Gawain and kissed him. And each evening, Gawain passed on the kisses to his host in return for the meat of the animal that Bertilak had killed on the hunt. On the third day, Bertilak's lady also persuaded Gawain to accept from her a green belt that she said would protect him from harm. Gawain tied the belt around his waist and hid it beneath his clothes. This he did not share with his host.

Gawain knew he needed to resume his search for the Green Chapel. So he asked for a guide and took his sad leave from his host and lady. The guide led Gawain deep into the forest, warning him that no one had ever survived a visit to the Green Chapel and urging him not to go

there. Gawain could not bear to think of himself committing a cowardly act, however—even if death was the certain consequence.

In a glade in the forest, Gawain found a green mound. The Green Knight emerged from a cave in the mound looking just as he had a year earlier, with his head back in place. At the giant's urging, Gawain removed his helmet and knelt down, waiting for the dreadful blow. The Green Knight swung his mighty ax and brought it down. Despite his efforts, Gawain flinched and the blow missed. The Green Knight mocked Gawain, who swore he would not flinch again.

So the Green Knight lifted the ax and swung again. This time, Gawain did not flinch, but again the blade missed. "Pray, sir, let us finish this," said Gawain. "Take your blow."

The Green Knight swung again, and this time the falling ax nicked Gawain's neck, drawing blood. At once, Gawain jumped up and pulled on his helmet. "I have received your blow," he said, "and so I am released from my penance."

"Indeed, sir," said the giant, "You are." "But let me ask, what was the meaning of your strange challenge in the first place?" asked Gawain.

The Green Knight explained that he was none other than the lord Bertilak, transformed by the sorceress Morgan le Fay (mawr guhn luh fay) to test the bravery of King Arthur's knights. The first two blows of his ax had been a recognition of the two days when Gawain had faithfully passed on the kisses from Bertilak's lady. The blow that drew blood was the result of Gawain deciding to keep the green belt.

Despite this, Bertilak hailed Gawain as the truest and bravest knight of them all. As Gawain left to return to Camelot, however, he decided to wear the green belt forever as a reminder of the occasion that his honesty had been tested—and he had been found wanting.

The World of
KING ARTHUR

Arthur is the main character in some of the most popular stories in world literature. For almost 1,000 years, writers have told of Arthur's brave deeds and the adventures of his knights of the Round Table. Storytellers passed on the earliest tales about Arthur by word of mouth in the 900's. These tales may have been based on an actual British leader who won minor victories over German invaders in the early A.D. 500's, but historians do not know much beyond that.

↑
King Arthur marries Princess Guenevere (GWEHN uh vihr), in an illustration from 1910.

The Holy Grail appears to the knights of the Round Table in a vision. In its earliest form in medieval legend, the Grail was a mysterious food-producing vessel.

The rocky headland of Tintagel in Cornwall (above) in southwestern England is one of many places identified as the possible site of Camelot (KAM uh lot), where King Arthur lived with his wife, Queen Guenevere. Arthur's table in this mighty castle was round so that all the knights ranked equally high. Other places identified with Camelot include Caerleon (kahr LEE uhn) Castle in Wales and Winchester (WIHN CHEHS tuhr) in southern England.

QUEST STORIES

Many of the stories about King Arthur and the knights of the Round Table involve dangerous journeys called quests. The knights undertook quests to find a specific object or to visit a particular location. The journey was the object of the story. The most famous of all the quests was the knights' search for the mystical Holy Grail, the cup said to have been used by Jesus Christ at the Last Supper.

The Green Knight's color and his association with the Green Chapel link him to the Green Man, a traditional English carving in which a human head is covered in vegetation (left). Green Man carvings appeared in English churches from around A.D. 400. They took the form of small gargoyles (GAHR goylz), which were covered in leaves or which sprouted leaves from their mouths, noses, or ears. They seem to be a symbol of the rebirth of nature in spring.

A VISION OF THE DEAD

For the ancient Scots, this story was a reminder that there is far more to the world than what we can see. Such stories may have helped struggling peasants feel more contented with their lives.

A poor woman from Nithsdale (NIHTHS dayl) sat spinning wool. Beside her, her child dozed in its cradle. Just then, the young mother heard a sound like dead leaves blowing in the wind. Turning to look, she saw a tall, beautiful lady dressed in green and carrying a baby.

"Would you please watch my baby until I return?" the Lady in Green asked. "Of course," replied the poor mother. The Nithsdale woman began to wonder when the Lady in Green did not return later that afternoon or that evening. She wondered even more the next day when she found new clothes for her children and some delicious cakes neatly arranged on the hearth.

Days passed, then months, and still the Lady in Green did not return. Summer arrived, and suddenly, the Lady in Green appeared again. A child on the floor reached for the hem of her dress, but its hand passed through the fabric. The strange woman was one of the aes sídhe (ees shee), fairy-kind!

"You have been most kind to my baby," said the Lady. "I'll take her now." "That is your right," the Nithsdale mother said, "but we've grown fond of her and will be sorry to part with her."

"Come with me," the Lady in Green said, "and I'll show you my house." They walked through the wood to a green hill. The Lady muttered strange words, and a door opened in the hill. They entered, and the door closed behind them. All the Nithsdale mother could see was bare dirt walls. But the Lady put three green drops in the mother's right eye.

"Now you see my home," said the Lady. The Nithsdale woman looked, and instead of bare walls, she saw a field of barley between green hills. A brook flowed through the field like a thread of silver. The Lady in Green put three green drops in the Nithsdale mother's left eye. This time when the mother looked, she saw people tending the fruit trees and harvesting barley. Some she recognized.

"I see many here I thought long dead!" exclaimed the mother. "What are they doing here?" "You see those who have died and now live in the Otherworld," said the Lady in Green.

Suddenly, the Nithsdale woman found herself back in the room with bare walls. For some time after, she could see the aes sídhe passing through the woods around her house. One day, she waved and said hello to one of the fairy-folk.

"With which eye do you see me?" asked the fairy. "With both eyes," the mother replied. The fairy blew into both her eyes and vanished. The Nithsdale woman never saw a fairy again.

The World of
THE ANCIENT SCOTS

Stories that described the lost world of the fairies may reflect Scotland's history. Ancient Scotland was inhabited by a people called Picts (pihkts) by the ancient Romans. The Latin word *pictor* means *painter*, and these people painted their skin (below). About A.D. 500, however, a Celtic tribe called the Scots from northern Ireland settled on Scotland's west coast. The Picts often dominated the Scots in the 700's and early 800's. But about 843, a Scottish king, Kenneth I MacAlpin, began ruling both peoples. The Picts ceased to exist as a separate people about A.D. 900.

Nithsdale (NIHTHS dayl) is the valley of the Nith River in the Scottish lowlands, near the border with England. The vision the Lady in Green shows the poor woman—of a rich land of fruit trees and barley— would have been a powerful one for farmers struggling to grow crops in the Scottish climate. The country often suffers cold, harsh weather. The lowlands were home to most of the population that spoke Gaelic (GAY lihk), a Celtic language.

THE IRISH CELTS IN SCOTLAND

In the past, waves of migrants traveled from Ireland's Ulster (UHL stuhr) area to Scotland's western highlands. They brought the Ulster and Fenian (FEE nee uhn) story cycles with them, which is why versions of these Irish stories also appear in Scots Gaelic.

The well-preserved stone ruins (left) at Skara Brae (skar uh bree) in Scotland's Orkney Islands represent one of the earliest settled communities in Europe. The mounds there are the remains of huts, built about 5,000 years ago using stone slabs. Each hut enclosed a single room with a central fireplace and a stone "dresser," which might have been used to display prized objects (above). The people who built the community, long before the Celts (kehlts) arrived, probably lived mainly by fishing. Skara Brae was abandoned about 2,500 years ago.

PWYLL AND

When the beautiful baby of King Pwyll and Queen Rhiannon was mysteriously stolen, Rhiannon was blamed for killing her own son.

King Pwyll (PWI lth) of Dyfed (DUH vehd) was at a feast when he saw a lady on a beautiful horse and said to a servant, "Ride out and ask who that lady is." No matter how hard the servant drove his steed, however, the lady seemed to get farther and farther away. The same thing happened again the next day.

On the third day, Pwyll mounted his swiftest steed and pursued the lady himself. But no matter how hard he rode, he could not catch the lady. "Lady! For the sake of love, please stop!" he shouted. Stopping, the lady said, "Gladly, but it would have been kinder to your horse to have asked sooner."

The lady was Rhiannon (hree AN on), a queen in the Otherworld, and she was seeking Pwyll as husband. "I will be given to a man I do not want unless you come to my father, Hyfaidd (hy fayd) the Old, in a year's time to claim me."

RHIANNON

A year later, Pwyll arrived at Hyfaidd's court to find a wedding feast already prepared. Food was served, and all made merry. A man approached Pwyll to ask a favor. "What do you wish?" asked Pwyll, "It's yours, if it's in my power to give!"

"Foolish man," hissed Rhiannon, "This is the man who wants my hand in marriage, and he will now ask it of you!"

"My name is Gwawl (GOO owl)," said the man, "and I ask that you give me Rhiannon and this feast."

Pwyll and Rhiannon took quiet counsel and created a plan. "Honor demands that I give Rhiannon to you," Pwyll said to Gwawl, "but the feast is Rhiannon's, not mine." "Meet me in a year's time, Gwawl," said Rhiannon, "and I and a feast will be prepared for you."

A year later, Gwawl and Rhiannon were sitting at the head of the table when Pwyll came before them disguised as a beggar. "Sir, I ask a favor on your day of happiness," said Pwyll. "So long as it is a modest favor," answered Gwawl.

Pwyll held out a small bag and said, "I ask only that you fill this bag with food." Gwawl agreed, unaware the bag had been enchanted by Rhiannon. It soon became obvious that the bag would not fill. Plate after plate entered the bag and still it was empty. "Will your bag never fill?!" cried Gwawl.

"Not until a lord stands upon it and says 'enough!'" said Pwyll.

Gwawl stood on the bag, but Pwyll tipped him inside and drew the strings tight. Pwyll's men then struck the bag with their sticks. "This is an unjust death for Gwawl," said Hyfaidd the Old. "Release him so long as he promises not to take any revenge."

Pwyll agreed, and then married Rhiannon. They returned to Dyfed and lived happily for three years. Then the nobles approached Pwyll and said, "Your wife has not produced an heir. Take another wife so we are sure to have a successor." "Wait a year," said Pwyll, "for things may change."

And indeed, Rhiannon was soon with child, and she bore a beautiful boy. Pwyll appointed six women to watch over

mother and child. But before midnight, all of them, including Rhiannon, had fallen asleep. In the morning, the women could not find the child. "Surely we will be hanged for this!" exclaimed one.

"Let us slaughter a puppy, smear its blood on Rhiannon's face, and place its bones next to her bed, saying she ate her child," said another. So they told this terrible lie about Rhiannon. In return, Rhiannon was forced to do penance. She had to sit at the gate of the castle, stop anyone who entered, and tell them the false story about what she had done. She then had to carry the people into the palace. This went on for years.

Meanwhile, there were strange happenings in nearby Gwent-is-Coed (gwehnt ihz koyd). Teyrnon (TEER nuhn), lord of that place, had a wonderful mare that gave birth to a beautiful foal at the end of May every year. Yet, by morning, the foal would be gone. Finally, Teyrnon decided to find out what happened to the foals.

The next year, as always, a beautiful foal was born. But this time, Teyrnon waited in the stable to see what would happen. At midnight, a large clawed arm reached in the window and grabbed the foal. Teyrnon drew his sword, hacked off the arm, and chased the monster away into the darkness.

When Teyrnon returned to the stable, he discovered a baby boy in the straw. He and his wife raised the child, calling him "Gwri (GOO ree) Golden-Hair," for his hair was the color of spun gold. But as the child grew, Teyrnon realized he was the very image of his true father, Pwyll. So he and his wife returned the child. Rhiannon met them at the gate, but her misery turned to joy at seeing the boy's likeness to Pwyll. Afterward, Rhiannon renamed her son Pryderi (prud AIR ee), which means *worry*, because of the distress he had caused his parents.

The World of
PWYLL AND RHIANNON

Pryderi (prud AIR ee) is widely known in Welsh mythology. His stories appear in a collection called *The Four Branches of the Mabinogi* (Maa bee noh gee). The circumstances of the birth of Pryderi are shrouded in mystery. Who or what takes him and places him in Teyrnon's (TEER nuhnz) manger? There doesn't seem any obvious purpose for Pryderi's kidnapping. Perhaps the story fulfills the typical mythological pattern in which the hero is separated from one or both parents at birth and is forced at an early age to develop the independence and other qualities that will distinguish him from all others.

Pwyll (PWI lth) catches up with Rhiannon (hree AN on) in a scene from the story of their meeting (above). Scholars do not know who wrote down the tales in *The Four Branches of the Mabinogi*. Since the mid-1800's, the four ancient tales in the *Mabinogi* have often been grouped with seven other early Welsh tales to form what is called the *Mabinogion* (maa bee noh gee ehn). King Arthur and his knights feast and fight (right) in paintings partly inspired by the *Mabinogion*.

Some modern-day Welsh are descended from prehistoric peoples who colonized Wales from continental Europe thousands of years ago. Many others trace their ancestry to such later settlers as the Romans, Anglo-Saxons, Vikings, Normans, and English.

The Welsh celebrate their ancient literary heritage at a festival called an eisteddfod (ay STEHTH vod). The traditions of Welsh literature date back more than 1,000 years to the bards (poet-singers) of the early Middle Ages. Until the end of the 1500's, many Welsh poets described the social life of their times, including preparations for war, raids, feasting, halls and castles, food and wine, and clothes and manners. They also described their relationships with other people.

DEITIES AND MYTHIC CHARACTERS OF ANCIENT BRITAIN AND IRELAND

aes sidhe (EYE shee)

The Irish term for fairies. They were often imagined as glowing, humanlike creatures living in a world parallel to ours. Tales depict them as doing great mischief.

Arthur

A legendary British king of the A.D. 400's and 500's, Arthur became king after drawing an enchanted sword from a stone. Guided by the magician, Merlin, he gathered the knights of the Round Table at his court in Camelot.

Balor (BAH lohr)

One-legged and one-eyed, Balor could kill with a stare. Told that his grandson would kill him, he locked his daughter in a crystal tower. But Cian found her and their union produced Lugh, the God of Craft.

Cian (KEE ahn)

Cian was a mighty warrior. Father to Lugh and grandfather to Cuchulainn, Cian was famous for his bravery.

Conchobar mac Nessa (KON cho var mak nessa)

King of Emain Macha, Conchobar gave Cuchulainn, then a child known as Sétanta, a home.

Cuchulainn (koo KUHL ihn)

Known both for his charm off the battlefield and fearsome deeds on it, Cuchulainn was an unstoppable force.

Originally named Sétanta, he changed his name after killing Culann's guard dog. After that, he stood in for the dog and guarded Culann's home and his flocks.

Dagda (DOY duh)

Known for his friendly disposition, Dagda was God of Life and Death. He had a magic staff that could kill nine men with one end and bring them back to life with the other.

Danu (DAHN oo)

Irish mother-goddess and founder of the Tuatha De Danaan tribe, Danu managed to be both mother of, and daughter to, Dagda. She was also Goddess of Wisdom and fertility.

Embarr (ehm bahr)

The horse of Manannán mac Mir, Embarr could gallop equally well over water and land.

Ethniu (EHN yuh)

Ethniu was the daughter of Balor and mother to Lugh. Her father locked her in a crystal tower to hide her from all men, but the cunning Cian still managed to find his way to her.

Finn MacCool

Known for his many dazzling deeds, Finn built the Giant's Causeway in Northern Ireland so he could meet a giant in Scotland for a duel. He was also father to Oisín.

Fomorians (foh MAHR ee uhnz)
Celtic gods and goddesses of chaos, the Fomorians came from the sea and were foiled in their attempt to conquer Ireland.

Gawain (guh WAYN)
King Arthur's nephew and one of the leading Knights of the Round Table, he was famous for his courage and loyalty in fighting the Green Knight.

Goibniu the Smith (GOY nee oo)
The metalworker god, Goibniu was official weapons supplier to the Tuatha De Danann, and uncle to Lugh.

Lugh (loo)
The handsome Celtic God of Crafts was thrown into the sea as a baby by his grandfather Balor, but was rescued by Manannán mac Lir, and grew to be famously brave; he managed in the end to kill Balor with a sling.

Maeve (mayv)
The queen of Connacht, Maeve tried to steal the Brown Bull of Cuailgne and was defeated in battle by Cuchulainn.

Manannán mac Lir (MAN an ahn mahk lihr)
God of the Sea and a renowned *helmsman* (pilot of a boat), Manannán was famous for his affairs with mortal women, and could change himself into a heron, or hide himself with his invisibility cloak.

Morgan le Fay
A powerful enchantress who tried to destroy King Arthur and the knights of the Round Table.

Niahm (nee ihv)
Niahm is the wife of Oisín, whom she takes to her father's magic kingdom.

Nuada (noo uh duh)
King of Tara, Nuada was a fearsome war god, until he lost his hand—and also the Kingdom of Ireland—in battle. His kind brother, Dian Cecht, forged him a new hand made from silver.

Oisín (uhsh EEN)
Poet and songwriter Oisín married Manannán mac Mir's daughter Niamh and went to live with her in the Land of Forever-Young. But on returning home to see his family, he discovered that centuries had passed and they were all long dead. When he touched the ground, he became an old man.

Pwyll (PWI lth)
Out hunting, King Pwyll unknowingly called off the stags belonging to the lord of the underworld and so denied that lord his sport. As punishment, he was forced to rule the underworld for a year. Later, he fell in love with and married Rhiannon.

Rhiannon (Hree AN on)
Wrongly accused by her husband Pwyll of eating their son, Pryderi, Queen Rhiannon suffered seven years of penance before the truth was discovered and her innocence established.

Sabdh (sive)
Changed into a fawn by an evil Druid, Sabdh was rescued by Finn MacCool and the power of true love.

Tuatha De Danann (too AH hah day dah NAHN)
Led by Dagda, this was the oldest family of Irish gods. They lived at first in the Western Isles, before moving to take up the task of fighting the Firbolgs, the Fomorians, and finally the Milesians.

GLOSSARY

alliteration The repetition of the same letter or sound at the start of two or more successive words.

alloy A metal created by mixing two other metals.

baptism Dipping a person into water or sprinkling a person with water, as a sign of the washing away of sin and of admission into the Christian church.

bard A poet who recites traditional verse, particularly long epics.

battle horn A musical instrument made from a cow's horn, blown to summon warriors into battle.

causeway A raised path across low or wet ground.

champion A skilled warrior who fights on behalf of a people.

cycle A series of poems or stories about the same theme.

Druids A class of Celtic priests, magicians, and fortunetellers.

enchanted Placed under a magic spell.

gargoyles Water spouts on a building, especially a church, that are carved into grotesque animal or human faces.

genre A style or type of literature or other form of art.

Holy Grail The cup or plate said to have been used by Jesus Christ at the Last Supper.

missionary A person sent to promote a religion, particularly Christianity, in a new country or region.

myth A traditional story that a people tell to explain their own origins or the origins of natural and social phenomena. Myths often involve gods, spirits, and other supernatural beings.

oath A solemn promise, usually made while calling on a form of god.

pagan Initially, individuals who worshiped the ancient Roman gods or the gods of such other ancient cultures. Over time, the term *pagan* came to describe a follower of almost any religion but Christianity.

penance A punishment by which a wrongdoer expresses public regret.

polytheistic Believing in a number of gods or goddesses at the same time.

prophecy A prediction of what will happen in the future.

quest A long or difficult search for something valuable.

ritual A solemn religious ceremony in which a set of actions is performed in a specific order.

sacred Something that is connected with the gods or goddesses and so should be treated with respectful worship.

sacrifice An offering made to a god or gods, often in the form of an animal or even a person who is killed for the purpose. Sacrifices also take the shape of valued possessions that might be buried, placed in caves, or thrown into a lake for the gods.

sling A weapon like a catapult for throwing small stones and rocks.

smite To strike extremely hard.

supernatural Describes something that cannot be explained by science or by the laws of nature, which is therefore said to be caused by beings such as gods, spirits, or ghosts.

FOR FURTHER INFORMATION

Books

Bernard, Catherine. *Celtic Mythology Rocks!* (Mythology Rocks!). Enslow Publishers, 2012.

Brezina, Corona. *Celtic Mythology* (Mythology Around the World). Rosen Central, 2008.

Cotterell, Arthur, and Rachel Storm. *The Ultimate Encyclopedia of Mythology.* Southwater, 2012.

Davies, Sioned. *The Mabinogion.* Oxford University Press, 2007.

Gagne, Tammy. *The Celts of the British Isles* (Explore Ancient Worlds). Mitchell Lane Publishers, 2013.

Green, Jen. *Ancient Celts: Archaeology Unlocks the Secrets of the Celts' Past* (National Geographic Investigates). National Geographic Society, 2008.

Green, Roger Lancelyn. *King Arthur and His Knights of the Round Table.* Puffin Classics, 2008.

Horowitz, Anthony. *Legends: Beasts and Monsters.* Kingfisher, 2010.

Massico, Katie. *What We Get From Celtic Mythology* (21st Century Skills Library: Mythology and Culture). Cherry Lake Publishing, 2015.

Matson, Glenna. *Celtic Mythology A to Z* (Mythology A to Z). Chelsea House Publishers, 2010.

Matthews, John. *King Arthur: Dark Age Warrior and Mythic Hero* (Prime Time History). Rosen Publishing Group, 2008.

Nardo, Don. *Celtic Mythology* (Mythology and Culture Worldwide). Lucent Books, 2014.

National Geographic Essential Visual History of World Mythology. National Geographic Society, 2008.

Philip, Neil. *Eyewitness Mythology* (DK Eyewitness Books). DK Publishing, 2011.

Rooney, Anne. *King Arthur and the Knights of the Round Table.* Carlton Books, 2009.

Websites

http://www.godchecker.com/pantheon/celtic-mythology.php
A directory of Celtic deities from God Checker, written in a light-hearted style but with accurate information.

http://www.pantheon.org/areas/mythology/europe/celtic/articles.html
Encyclopedia Mythica page with links to many pages about Celtic deities in the left-hand column.

http://www.pantheon.org/areas/folklore/arthurian/articles.html
Encyclopedia Mythica page with links to many pages about Arthurian legend in the left-hand column.

http://www.mythome.org/celtic.html
A page with links to many Celtic gods and goddesses and elements of Celtic culture.

http://www.crystalinks.com/celts.html
This Crystal Links page has links to articles about all aspects of ancient Celtic history and mythology.

INDEX

PRONUNCIATION KEY	
Sound	**As in**
a	hat, map
ah	father, far
ai	care, air
aw	order
aw	all
ay	age, face
ch	child, much
ee	equal, see
ee	machine, city
eh	let, best
ih	it, pin, hymn
k	coat, look
o	hot, rock
oh	open, go
oh	grow, tableau
oo	rule, move, food
ow	house, out
oy	oil, voice
s	say, nice
sh	she, abolition
u	full, put
u	wood
uh	cup, butter
uh	flood
uh	about, ameba
uh	taken, purple
uh	pencil
uh	lemon
uh	circus
uh	labyrinth
uh	curtain
uh	Egyptian
uh	section
uh	fabulous
ur	term, learn, sir, work
y	icon, ice, five
yoo	music
zh	pleasure